Forgiven,

Healed,

and

Restored

Dionysus Publications
10 North Church Street
Greenville SC 29601

Maynard, Dennis R, 1944-
Forgiven, Healed, and Restored

Library of Congress Catalog Card Number: 94-092276
ISBN 1-885985-01-0

Suggested Dewey classification - 234 Ma

Suggested LC classification - BT795.M39 1994
Subjects:
1. Forgiveness of sin.
2. Healing — Religious aspects.
3. Guilt — Religious aspects.
4. Theology.

Forgiven, Healed, and Restored

Dennis R. Maynard

Dionysus Publications
Greenville SC

Other titles
by
Dennis Maynard

Those Episkopols (1994)
(ISBN 1-885985-02-9)

The Money Book (1994)
(ISBN 1-885985-00-2)

Forgiven, Healed, and Restored was typeset on a Macintosh© Quadra 800 Computer using *Pagemaker 5.0* © . The cover design was also done on a Macintosh Quadra 800 Computer using *TypeStyler 2.0* ©.

Table of Contents

Foreword

He had been caught in an act of adultery! Now he sat in my office in a puddle of tears. Great sobs shook his body. He had been married for fifteen years. This was the first time he had ever been unfaithful. He was the father of two children. Because his affair had been with a coworker he had lost his job with the company. His wife would not forgive him. She had hired the "meanest and greediest divorce attorney in the city." She was going after him for all she could get.

I had heard his confession. I believed his contrition was real. The other woman had reconciled with her husband. They had moved to a distant city. He had told me of his loneliness. He talked of his wife's indifference. He and the other woman had started out as friends. Nothing more. Then they found they had so much in common. They could talk for hours. They looked forward to being together. And then one thing led to another.

Still, he loved his wife. He was sorry. He wanted them to get into counseling. He wanted to begin again. And then there were more tears. He would never be able to forgive himself.

"God forgives you," I told him, "and I forgive you. Your friends and your family forgive you, and this Church forgives you. Now you must learn to forgive yourself."

He then grew very angry as he shouted at me. "No, Padre, you are the only one who has forgiven me. Our friends won't talk to me. I came to church last Sunday and people just sneered at me and whispered. Even our former priest won't return my phone calls. He has ignored the letters I have written him. How can I forgive myself when the people who said that they loved me won't forgive me?"

His wife's attorney prevailed. She got him for most everything he had, including full custody of the two children. He lost everything. He quit coming to church, and after a time, I lost touch with him.

I have thought about that man on several occasions. He has especially come to mind when I have been called on to minister to other men and women caught in adultery or some other public sin. I have always felt like we failed him. We preached forgiveness. We prayed forgiveness. We gave him absolution, but the Church never made the forgiveness real. Those who called themselves Christians never forgave him as they were forgiven.

If you and I in the Church don't make the words of forgiveness come to life, they are only words. If we Christians fail to incarnate the words of forgiveness we utter Sunday by Sunday, then they are but empty cliches. Could it be that when it comes to forgiveness, the Church is no more than a noisy gong or a clanging cymbal?

A priest friend of mine has said that in the Church today everything is permitted, but nothing is forgiven. I find it ironic that at the very same time our church is debating whether or not to ordain practicing homosexuals, we have implemented background checks on church employees. Regardless of how you feel about that proposal, do you not see the irony?

I fear that we have become a church that has been entrusted with the power to forgive sins, but we have forgotten how. We can utter the words with ease. We have forgotten how to manifest them in our lives and in our communities.

This book is a collection of reflections I did for our parish paper on forgiveness. This book has been written to call the leaders of our church back to the ministry of reconciliation. This book is filled with the promise of healing for those who have been wounded by their own sins or the sins of others. The pain is real, but so is the prescription.

I think there is one question every church leader needs to ask him or herself. If you were a penitent, ordained or lay, truly sorry for your sins, wanting to amend your life, and follow again the commandments of Jesus — would you confess your sins to this church? If the answer is no, whether it be for fear of retribution or being held up as a bad example, the condemnation falls not on the penitent, but on those who have been given the authority to forgive sins.

My fear is that in the current climate, our church is beginning to sound more vindictive than forgiving. Our message sounds more hurtful than healing, our example more alienating than reconciling. The way we have destroyed the lives and ministries of some of our own members is a far greater sin than those of the accused.

This book is entitled *Forgiven, Healed, and Restored* because the ministry of reconciliation involves all three. To forgive is only the first step. There then must be healing. The pain, the hurt, and the anger caused by the act of sin have to be put away and remembered no more. But, reconciliation is not complete until there is restoration. This is the third and most difficult step.

Those who are truly repentant and seek to be reconciled to the community are not brought back into the fold as second class citizens. No, to be restored to the household of God is to be restored with all the rights and privileges of a full member of the family.

By far the third step in reconciliation may be the most difficult for us to incarnate. Forgiveness without it, however, is just as incomplete as repentance without amendment of life. Just as repentance must be complete, so must reconciliation. For a penitent merely to mouth the words of confession is but a form of cheap grace. For the Church to merely mouth the words of absolution cheapens the grace of God just as dramatically.

Every penitent cries out in prayer to be forgiven, to have the hurt they have caused healed, and to be restored to the Household of Faith. Our world desperately needs a church in which the wounds of life can be healed. These wounds cannot be healed with lip service. The community of reconciliation must be a place where people can experience the healing we proclaim.

I once heard a bishop say that eighty percent of the people seeing psychiatrists ought to be seeing priests. Their pain, he reasoned, was guilt. They need to hear the words of forgiveness. This book not only reminds us of Jesus' words of forgiveness, but of our need to make it possible for hurting people to experience them.

Acknowledgments

I am grateful to all who first read these chapters and encouraged me to have them published. To the many members of Christ Church Parish in Greenville, South Carolina, who have continued to encourage me in my writings, I am most grateful.

I am equally grateful to the members of the clergy and the Bishops from throughout our Church who also encouraged me to put these writings in a book.

Thanks to a gift from Lila, Ashley, Rory, and Rob Payne, the initial costs for publishing this manuscript were covered. They gave their gift for this purpose in memory of Blair Smoak, Lois Clark, and Steve Griffeth.

This book would not have been possible without the tireless efforts of Bill and Barbara Scott, who not only prepared it for publication, but read and re-read it. Their suggestions, encouragement, and assistance kept me going.

Dennis Maynard
Greenville, South Carolina
August, 1994

Chapter One

This Book Is For You

If you lay awake at night feeling the sting of unfair criticism, the hurt of the gossip monger, or the memory of being hurt by another person's sharpness, then this book is for you.

If you have known sleepless nights because of another person's betrayal, callousness, or insensitivity, then this book is for you.

If you have been the object of ridicule or discrimination because of your race, sex, age, height or weight, then this book is for you.

If you have suffered the indignity of verbal or physical abuse; if you have been humiliated by another who chose to use their position, wealth, or status to control and manipulate you; if you have ever been reminded of your "place," then this book is for you.

If you, a family member, or your house has ever been violated by another's greed, attempts to rape, steal, or murder, then this book is for you.

If you have ever been on the receiving end in marriage, family, friendship, business, or church of another's intentional violations of the commandments of God, of things done, said, and left undone, then this book is for you.

This book is about our need to set apart a time for prayer and fasting, committed to forgiving those who have injured us. It is about letting go of the sting. This book encourages us to leave the past in the past and resolve never to bring it to the present again. This book is about letting go of the hurts that continue to take their toll on our bodies and our souls. It is about beginning again.

But, this book is also about coming to terms with ourselves. It is about honest self-examination. It is about trying to understand the hurt that our own insensitivities, betrayals, and disobedience have brought to the lives of those who have trusted us and believed in us.

If you have ever looked with envy on another person's life, position, wealth, happiness, spouse or children, then this book is for you.

If you have ever expressed your own inner pain with words of criticism, gossip, innuendo, or accusation against another, then this book is for you.

If you have ever used your position, wealth, or status to control or manipulate others, and thus keep them in their place, then this book is for you.

If you have ever wished that another person no longer existed, were not in your life, or otherwise murdered them in your mind, then this book is for you.

If you have ever looked with lust on another person and longed for a way to fulfill that fantasy, then this book is for you.

If you have taken delight in the sins of others and determined that neither they nor anyone else would ever forget them, then this book is for you.

This book encourages us to repent of our own sins. It encourages us to amend our ways and live a new life in Christ Jesus by becoming a new person. It encourages us to make it our intention to never hurt another person in thought, word, deed, or neglect. It reminds us that we are forgiven exactly as we forgive.

This book is serious business. This book is at the heart of what it is to be a Christian. This book is for people just like you and me. This book, my friends, is for us!

Chapter Two

Proper Folks Don't Sin

When I was a kid, there was a teacher in our school by the name of Miss Frey. Miss Frey was the most proper lady I had ever met. Miss Frey knew how to stand and sit in the proper way. Miss Frey knew how to speak properly and walk properly. Her favorite word was "proper." Miss Frey taught Manners Classes after school!

We all knew that sooner or later we were going to end up in Miss Frey's Manners Classes. There Miss Frey would teach us all the things that a proper young gentleman should know. Miss Frey was quite concerned that her young gentlemen hold up the proper image.

I was thinking not too long ago how difficult sin and repentance must be on proper people. In order to confess one's sins, one has to admit they have not behaved in a proper manner. They must confess to having made a mistake. No proper person would ever consciously make a mistake.

I think the public sinner has the advantage over proper folks when it comes to sin and repentance. The town drunk knows that he is the town drunk. He knows that everyone knows he is the town drunk. The president of the Garden Club, however, must live daily with her little secret. The adulterer who has been publicly revealed knows that he or she is an adulterer, and now everyone else knows it as well. The civic leader lives with the fear of being discovered.

Repentance is easier for those who already are conscious of their imperfections. Proper folks are at a distinct disadvantage.

Not long ago I was interviewing a person for a position at our church. I asked, "When was the last time you made a mistake, and what did you learn from it?" This very proper person thought for a moment and then replied, "I can't remember making a mistake." Proper people have never learned to live with the discontent of their imperfections. Then, again, maybe proper people don't have a high enough standard.

There is the story of the minister who went to see a lady in his congregation. She had not been very active. The minister began, "When you take an active role in our congregation you bring so many gifts with you. We are better for your presence. What on earth can I say to you to get you to be a little more active in the life of our church?"

The woman's eyes widened, and she responded, "Oh, Father, you don't understand. I don't want to be that good. I just want to be good enough to stay out of hell when I die!"

There are the Hollywood Sins of sex, drugs, booze, and money. No proper person would ever succumb to one of these. When one does, it is not seen so much as a sin, but as a disgrace. Such behavior brings shame on the entire family.

There are, however, other sins that don't always make the tabloids, but can be every bit as devastating . Control, manipulation, greed, sloth, bigotry, and arrogance are but a few. These, however, are not sins in the eyes of good proper folk. Control and manipulation are simply looking out for what is best for everyone. Bigotry is not giving people more privilege or responsibility than they can handle. And arrogance, oh, that's simply maintaining the family lineage, displaying the degrees on the wall, or belonging to the right clubs.

I fear that acknowledgment of sin and repentance must be very difficult for proper people. The public sinner does have the advantage. Perhaps that is the reason the public sinners were so responsive to the teachings of Jesus. Perhaps that is the reason the proper religious folks in His day took such offense to Him.

It is sad to think that things really haven't changed all that much. Those of us who know that we need a Savior can't seem to get enough of this Jesus-Loves-Me talk. And, just as in days gone by, there are those proper church folk who continue to be most distressed over the proper seasonal colors, proper placement of the flowers on the altar, getting proper church members and finding proper clergy to serve them.

The challenge for the Church today in this respect is identical to the challenge that Jesus faced. We must not let the proper religious folk keep us from ministering to those in need of healing. God sends into every congregation people who need to hear Christ's words of comfort and forgiveness. They are the sheep without a shepherd. In their pain, they have no desire to get involved in whatever the latest parish squabble might be. They are people in pain in search of a physician. On occasion, in order to make room for Jesus, we may have to ask the proper religious folk to simply stand aside.

The Church is for sinners. Proper religious folk have a difficult time accepting that.

Chapter Three

What Will People Say?

Recently I read this statement. "When man discovered the mirror, he lost his soul." The suggestion is that, at that point, we became more concerned about our images than the health of our souls. The image consultants can give each of us pointers on how to "look the part." Dressing for success, sitting correctly, smiling at appropriate times, and having a firm handshake are all critical to keeping up appearances.

The mirror image we want to present to the world is one of people who are quite proper. We are a people in control, without problems, very successful, and extremely happy. The one acceptable alternative to being happy is being intensely concerned (angry) about a particular cause.

I find it interesting that, in my lifetime, two of the best read books on sin have been written by psychiatrists, not by theologians. Karl Menninger, M.D., wrote a book with a most descriptive title, *Whatever Happened to Sin?* This book takes the masks off our efforts to make acts of sin appear more socially acceptable.

The second book I have in mind is equally revealing. It, too, was written by a psychiatrist: Scott Peck, M.D., wrote *People of the Lie*. Again, our efforts to always appear to be in charge, proper, and/or justified can be used as a coverup for a host of sinful, even evil behaviors.

The fact that religious piety can also be used as a coverup for sin and evil is a reality that must be confronted. Historically, in the name of Jesus, wars have been fought, people have been oppressed, and great evil has been done. Today, people may hide behind religious piety to express their "concerns" about church, clergy, and fellow church members. Such masks can be worn to disguise slander, prejudice, bigotry, envy, and a host of other lies as religious or at least righteous causes.

"When man discovered the mirror, he became more concerned about his image than the health of his soul." The impression we make on one another does carry some import. What people think of us is of some value.

Beyond what people think, however, is a much more critical concern. "What does God think?" The Holy One knows the secrets of our hearts. We may be successful in currying the favor of family, friends, and fellow church members. Our images may be intact, but if it is all a charade, then it is the worst form of hypocrisy.

Each year the Church begins the Season of Lent with a service on *Ash Wednesday*. It is a very dangerous service. It is a penitential service. The liturgy is designed primarily for those who are more concerned about their soul's health than their image. People who attend *Ash Wednesday* services participate in a liturgy that calls us to repent of our sins, to confess them, and promise to amend our lives.

This is a most dangerous service because it is for people who understand that they are sinners. They are publicly admitting that they have sinned in thought, word, deed, and omission. This means the masks of propriety, success, and religious piety have to be removed.

A word of caution must be given. If you choose to attend an *Ash Wednesday* service, you will be seen! The services are for sinners. Your anonymity cannot be guaranteed. However, you can take comfort in the fact that you will be seen primarily by other people who see themselves as sinners as well.

Chapter Four

Give Me An Honest-To-God Sinner

There was a lot of tension in the room. We had gathered in a workshop format a few years ago to discuss one of the resolutions to come before Diocesan Convention. The resolution itself had pretty evenly divided the Convention. A priest stood to speak to the resolution. "I have broken every commandment of God," he began. "I have committed the sin of fornication. I have lied and stolen what belonged to another. I committed adultery, and that sin contributed to my first marriage ending in divorce. While fighting in Viet Nam, I committed murder. I am a sinner. I have grieved over my sins. I continue to suffer the consequences of my sins. As a sinner I cannot support a resolution that singles out one sin as more grievous than another. I cannot pretend self-righteousness. I cannot sit in judgment on others."

I looked at the priest sitting next to me, "What do you think about what he said?"

He glared at me, "I think he should be deposed! He should not be a priest."

"Funny," I responded. "I was thinking we should make him Presiding Bishop!"

To which my pew mate replied, "You're out of your mind, Maynard."

Perhaps I am, but I continue to give thought to the people in my life who have taught me the most about being a Christian. I find that my own spiritual journey has been strengthened most not by the saints, but by repentant sinners. By sinners, I don't mean the "gosh! I wasn't very nice, was I?" sinners. I mean the "honest-to-God, I messed up big time" sinners.

Those who find themselves guilty of violating church etiquette, but otherwise having lived a virtuous existence, have not helped me much. The self righteous, having been guilty only of minor infractions, have not taught me much of anything. I would never seek such a person out for guidance, let alone confession.

No, give me an honest-to-God sinner every time. I want one who has come to terms with the consequences of his or her behavior. Give me one who has experienced the pain of separation from God. Show me a sinner who realizes the pain his or her acts of sin have caused others. That is someone who can teach us something.

Alcoholics Anonymous has a leg up on us in the Church. In the Church we look for people who can give the appearance of living sinless lives to hold up as role models. AA looks for drunks who can help other drunks. When will we ever learn? Only a sinner can help another sinner.

The hymn *O, for a closer walk with God* includes this prayer:

> Where is the blessedness I knew when first I saw the Lord?
> Where is the soul refreshing view of Jesus and His word?
> Return, O holy Dove, return sweet messenger of rest;
> I hate the sins that made thee mourn, and drove thee from my breast.

The honest-to-God repentant sinner has prayed that prayer in one form or another. They have experienced separation from God and from self. They have longed for reunion. They can teach us, counsel us, guide us in a way that those who pretend to have no sin never can. Like Paul (*Romans 6:15*), I am not suggesting that there should be more sin so there could be more grace. No, I would just have us be reminded that the primary message of the Gospel is repentance and not image maintenance. The primary consideration for all Christians is to come to terms with one's sins and not perpetuate a mask of perfection.

The person who can say, "I have broken every commandment of God either in thought, word, or deed," seems to me to have a leg up spiritually on the professional church worker who is guilty only of occasional ecclesiastical improprieties.

I believe the following statement is attributed to an elderly nun: "God, deliver me from saints. I know it will be wonderful to rejoice in their fellowship in heaven, but here on earth they can be so difficult to live with."

Chapter Five

The Sins We Do Not See

When a new Rector is installed, the Prayer Book instructs that at the service celebrating the new ministry, the Rector kneel before the congregation and offer the following prayer. "O Lord my God, I am not worthy to have you come under my roof; yet you have called your servant to stand in your house, and to serve at your altar." (*BCP 562*) Every new ministry then begins with the Rector's confession of unworthiness.

I am painfully aware of many of my sins. The sting of some of them causes me to shudder to this very day. I am painfully aware that there is not a single commandment of God that I have not broken in one way or another. While it has been years, even decades, since I have repented of some of these sins, the memory of many of them still haunts me in the stillness of the night.

The sins that I fear most, however, are not those of which I am conscious, but the sins that I do not see. I fear my sins of omission — the things I have left undone — the sins of nice people. I fear the number of times that I have let another person down and not known it. I fear the times that I have tried to be cute at another's expense but did not see that I had cut them to the heart. I fear the number of things I have left undone because I was preoccupied with that which was not nearly so important. I fear the times that I have tried to build myself up at the expense of another. To know one's sins, to acknowledge and confess one's sins, this is the pathway to reconciliation. But what about those sins that we do not see?

Perhaps if Adam and Eve had simply acknowledged their wrongdoing in the garden, everything would be different today. If only they had owned up to their act of rebellion. "Yes, Lord, we did it. We knew it was wrong. Please forgive us." Those are the words that bring healing. Adam and Eve didn't; and so today, we know that through one man's fall we all sin.

Daily we can strive to be better and do better. Daily we can reach for the standard that eludes us. Daily we can examine our consciences and see clearly the mistakes we have made. And daily we must live with the knowledge that in spite of our best efforts we have not been perfect and the sins that we see and the ones that we do not see convict us.

Professor William Muel of Yale Divinity School has stated, "Imperfection is not the corruption of history, it is the essence of history." Our cries for a perfect world blessed by a perfect Church filled with perfect people flies in the face of reality.

The pop psychologist reminds us that the gospel is not "I'm O.K., You're O.K." The gospel of Jesus Christ is, "I'm not O.K., and You're not O.K, but through the Cross of Christ, we are O.K."

The village philosopher reminds us that the reason they put erasers on the end of pencils is because people make mistakes. Still, all the words of comfort from theologian, psychologist, and philosopher cannot remove the sting that we have inflicted on others or on ourselves. The rebellion of Adam and Eve has had a ripple effect throughout the pages of history. The sins that we both see and don't see are a part of the history of the people's lives we have both touched and failed to touch.

The comforting words for me are found in the knowledge that with the rest of humanity I am on a journey. A journey that will not find its completion in a single day. Repentance and forgiveness are the essential ingredients in this journey. Day by day God leads us toward Himself and the fulfillment of the longing of our souls. This journey of repentance and forgiveness might best be summarized in the prayer of an elderly black woman, "Lord, I know that I am not all that I am suppose to be. And Lord, I know that I am not yet what I am gonna be. But Lord, I sure thank you that I am not what I used to be. Amen."

Chapter Six

How We Crucify Jesus Today

You know it will be a bad day when you arrive home and the crew from *60 Minutes* is waiting for you in your driveway. It seems that corporate America is in agreement. A recent survey of 110 of the 1,000 Fortune companies confirmed that the senior executives were not crazy about broadcast journalism in general. They listed *60 Minutes* as the primary television show they would **not** want to do a report on their company. Also listed were *A Current Affair* and *Hard Copy*.

It is one thing to have the tabloid journalists turn their attention to our competitor, leading candidates, office holders in the opposing parties, a community or Church leader, or even a neighbor. It is quite another to think about being the target of these investigations.

Tabloid journalism is not new. As we read the gospel accounts of the trial of Jesus, we will see the entire event has a lot to do with sleaze tactics, character assassination, innuendo, and destructive gossip. Each time I read the accounts of our Lord's Passion, I like to assign myself one of the heroic roles. I'd like to think that I would have been one of those who defended Jesus. "Leave Him alone!" I would shout. "Look at all the good that He has done. He has healed, and comforted, and taught, and forgiven." Or perhaps, I would be Simon of Cyrene carrying the cross of my Lord. At the very least I would be John who would be comforting the women and praying for Jesus.

Yes, we all would want to wear a white hat at the crucifixion of our Lord. Truth is, however, we most likely would play the role we play today whenever the tabloid journalists, or trouble makers, or gossip mongers turn their sights on another person. There are many roles to play: there are, of course, those who lead the pack; those who must go though the garbage heap of the past looking for incriminating evidence; those who would take the innocent words, remarks, and statements of another and then turn this information back on them. Jesus' accusers did this very thing — "He (Jesus) said that, 'He was ...,' or 'would do...,' or 'is...' "

Then there were those unhappy with their own lives — those who had hearts filled with envy; those who were jealous of the love the crowds gave Jesus. They shouted out of their own torment, "Crucify Him! Get rid of Him! He has done it to Himself. He is getting what He deserves."

There were also those who simply lurked in the background. "What have you heard now?" "Do you know what I heard?" "I understand that His parents were not even married." "What do you expect of someone from Galilee?"

Those who participated in the rumor mongering and the verbal speculation were every bit as guilty of crucifying Jesus as those who actively worked to trump up the charges against Him.

Then there were the silent. Those who said nothing. Those who watched with idle curiosity waiting to see which way the wind would blow. "What a shame," they would say shaking their heads. "Religious people should not behave that way." But they would say nothing. They would do nothing. They could have spoken out on His behalf, but they did not. They are condemned by their silence.

Some would simply deny Him. Cowards all. "He was never my friend." "I really didn't know Him all that well." "No, you must be mistaken. I never really liked Him."

We would all like to think that we would have been one of the heroes. We would have defended Jesus. We would have spoken on His behalf. The harsh truth is that at the execution of Jesus our role most likely would resemble the role we play today when another person is being crucified in the press or among the gossip mongers. The words of Jesus need to haunt us in light of the current climate in the Church and our nation, "Whatever you do unto the least of the brethren, you have done unto me."

Whenever we actively or passively participate in the crucifixion of another person's character, career, or life, we are reliving the role we would have played in our Lord's crucifixion. When we agree to the crucifixion of another, we in fact crucify Jesus. Father, forgive us.

Chapter Seven

All Sin Is Sin

What does one say about the terrible cruelties we hear about daily in the news? I only have to mention the name Jeffrey Dahmer and I need no further illustration. There are other serial murderers and rapists. Then there are the mass murderers and those in the sacred positions of priests, counselors, teachers, and parents who abuse the children, young people, and adults entrusted to their charge. How does the gospel of forgiveness apply to these people? What would Jesus say to them?

I asked a psychiatrist, a psychologist, and a prison social worker to review this chapter. What I have learned is first that there are those individuals who truly have a pathological need to do that which they do. Some professionals think the genetic engineering of these people is all fouled up. Others think it may be chemical or even hormonal. Yet, others believe that it is environmental.

Those who were raised in abusive atmospheres often end up being abusive. Some think it is a combination of all of the previously mentioned.

The bottom line, however, is that these people appear to be "possessed" with the desire to do that which they do. There is little that we can do for them except restrain them so that they cannot harm anyone else.

Perhaps it was people like this who Jesus tried to exorcise of their demons. Today, there are few exorcists, and there appears to be little hope for changing the possessed's behavior, putting an end to the unbelievable terror they wreak on their victims.

To ask those who have been the victims to have compassion on their tormentors stretches our understanding of grace, but stretch we must.

I have learned that there are others who again, through no fault of their own, suffer from addictions. We most commonly think of the alcoholic, but the list of addictions is lengthy. Drugs, food, gambling, sex, work, credit buying, etc. These obsessive-compulsive types may also have a defective gene, a chemical or hormonal imbalance.

The pain they often cause themselves and others is real. The most successful treatment has been the various twelve-step programs. The success rate, while impressive, is not one hundred percent. If these folks can take responsibility for their own recovery and work on a spiritual life plan, there is hope. Again, forgiving these people the pain they have caused family members and others is a part of the Christian journey. *Tough Love* is often the only type of love that can get them started on the recovery process.

There are still others who suffer from other forms of pathology. There is the compulsive liar who will lie to you when the truth would serve his or her purpose better, the kleptomaniac, the voyeur, the philanderer, and others again who just can't seem to help themselves. Perhaps it is a faulty gene, a chemical imbalance, hormones. Whatever it is, they, too, bring pain to others. We shall never completely be able to understand the hysteria that drives families, tribes, gangs, entire nations to try to annihilate one another.

There is one final group in the Psychiatric Handbook that I found interesting. These are the folks who have no concept of any imperfections in themselves. Like the Pharisees of old, they are without sin. These are so wrapped up in keeping up an image of propriety that they are completely oblivious to the pain they cause others. It was of these that psychiatrist Scott Peck wrote in *People of the Lie*.

Like the ancient Pharisees, these are often proper, religious folk, but they have no need of forgiveness since they have kept all the rules and are without sin. (Or they are without any sin worthy of discussion.) The sadness is that these people are often "mean spirited," creating havoc wherever they go, but have deluded themselves into believing that they are the good people trying to do what they think is in the best interest of those they are attempting to help.

This business of forgiving others has to take into account the mental capacity of those who have harmed us. Obviously, to seek forgiveness for ourselves requires a conscience that refuses to condone the choices we have made. It appears that, for whatever reason, some folks are incapable of asking forgiveness for themselves. We, however, are called always to be forgiving. Our own soul's health is dependent on our perfecting this capacity in response to the grace of God at work within each of us.

Chapter Eight

Shoot The Wounded

Our junior high school shop teacher had given us an assignment. We were to memorize the procedure for bringing a board to square. We were to be examined the following week. Any student who failed to memorize the procedure was to be brought before the class and given one swat with a wood paddle. The teacher had such a paddle hanging on the wall behind his desk. I feel certain that he had lovingly brought it to square using the proper procedure. The following week well over half the class had failed to memorize the procedure. The teacher made good on his threat. One by one the boys were brought to the front of the class, told to bend over and grab their ankles. Each received a well placed swat on the behind from the shop teacher. This went on for several weeks as the number of swats increased in proportion to the number of days the student failed to master the assignment.

The Church, at its very worst, has studied in that shop teacher's school of theology. The way to motivate people to do right is to threaten them with punishment, humiliation, and pain. When folks fail to live up to the standard, then excommunicate them or make a public example out of them just in case there are any others thinking about doing the same.

The Church at its best, however, has remembered that sin is not a crime to be punished but a disease to be healed. The Church at its best has seen the destructive nature of the sin, but has also seen the pain of the sinner. The Church at its best has realized that any army that insists on shooting its wounded, even when those wounds are self-inflicted, will soon be short on new recruits. The good news of the Gospel is that "God did not send His Son into the world to condemn the world, but that through Him the world might be saved." (*John 3:16*)

There is the true story of a young woman who was very active in her church. She was a leader in the local youth program and that of the diocese. She also had a boyfriend. They were very much in love. They were not very careful and she became pregnant. She dropped out of her church activities. Her Rector went to see her to try to get her to return, but she was convinced she would be subjected to the disdain of the congregation.

Some of the women in the congregation heard about her plight and decided they wanted to give her a baby shower. Others heard about their plan and got very upset with them. "What kind of message will you be sending the rest of our young people if you do that? You'll be telling them that we approve of that sort of thing." Those planning the shower persisted. They knew exactly the type of message they wanted to send to that young woman and the other young people in their congregation. Jesus did not come to condemn and to punish, but to redeem.

The wind and the sun were having a contest as to who was the mightiest. The wind said, "You see that man walking across that bridge? I will get his coat off him in less time than you can." So the wind blew gust after gust at the man, but with each successive gust the man only clutched his coat all the more tightly to his body. Then it came the sun's turn. The sun simply begin to shine on the man. The sun bathed the man in the warmth of its radiance. Soon the man voluntarily took off his coat.

Those who already are gripped by their own shame, kept by their own secrets, and suffering with the pain of their own self-inflicted wounds are not going to come to a church that shoots its wounded. There will not be many volunteering for public humiliation and embarrassment. Jesus Christ did not so treat the sinners of His day and neither should His Church. Those who are already suffering need no additional wounds. They will respond to being bathed in the warmth of God's love. You and I can be the instruments that make that love real for them. We simply must make sure our church is sending the right message.

Chapter Nine

Marked For Life

In Galveston, Texas, there is a souvenir shop out on the pier. That shop has been there for at least forty years. I know. When I was about eight years old, I went in that shop with my parents. There was a little pocket knife I wanted. My parents refused to buy it for me. I wandered away from them and I took it! My parents caught me, made me take it back and apologize.

With the current spirit in our nation, I am glad that the Board of Examining Chaplains didn't know that story. Otherwise, I would probably not be ordained today. I would be marked for life as a thief who is not to be trusted.

The Spiritual Directors make a distinction between *Habitual Sins* and a *Sin of the Occasion*. *Habitual Sins* become a way of life. *Sins of the Occasion* are those singular acts when we know that we are doing wrong, but we do it anyway. I should suspect that if the theft of a knife in a souvenir store at an early age were to be followed by yet other thefts, followed by a life of burglaries, armed robberies, or the white collar crimes of fraud and embezzlement, then any review board would have reason to wonder.

This distinction between *Habitual Sins* and *Sins of the Occasion* needs to be reconsidered. If a Baby Boomer candidate for office confesses he or she smoked a marijuana cigarette at an early age, there are those who want to quickly label that candidate a drug addict and not trustworthy. Does this, in fact, stand up to logic? Because a person has a history of alcohol abuse, does that mean that they should not be given a position of responsibility for fear that they might relapse into their old ways? I have often seen a husband or wife reconcile with an unfaithful spouse and then live out a long marriage of fidelity. And, I have seen the adulterous spouse leave one marriage and enter another, never to have the sin repeated. A person can do bad things (sin). This does not necessarily make them a bad person. The Gospel does not fill the repentant with shame but with cleansing.

I admit to having a singular flaw. I believe in redemption. I believe in the healing power of Jesus Christ. I believe people can change and be changed. I do not believe in marking folks for life because a temptation of the past overwhelmed them.

If a behavior is pathological, then that is another matter. Those who see theft, adultery, addictions, etc., as a way of life need a different kind of scrutiny. The message of repentance is directed to those who pray with the Psalmist, "I know my transgressions, and my sin is ever before me. Create in me a clean heart, O God, and put a new and right spirit within me." (*Psalm 51*).

As the Church of Jesus Christ we hold before the people of the world a message of redemption. To all people convicted of their sins we proclaim that we are a community of reconciliation. Here people are given the opportunity to begin again. Their *Sins of Occasion* are forgiven and they are "restored to the fellowship of the Church. Thereby, the whole congregation was put in mind of the message of pardon and absolution set forth in the Gospel of our Savior, and of the need which all Christians continually have to renew their repentance and faith." (*BCP 265*). I find nothing in the Scriptures that directs us to mark folks for life because of their *Sins of Occasion*.

I love the story of the little girl who told her parish priest that she had been talking to God and she could hear God talk back. The priest reported it to the Bishop. The Bishop told the little girl that the next time she talked to God, have God list for her the sins that the Bishop had uttered at his last confession.

Weeks passed and the Bishop asked the little girl, "Did you talk to God?" She replied that she had. The Bishop asked if she had requested that God list the Bishop's sins for her. She answered that she had.

"And what did God say?" the Bishop inquired.

The little girl smiled and stated, "God said that He forgot."

God forgets our sins. He remembers them no more. He does not label us for life because of our past offenses. By what authority would we dare to label one another?

Chapter Ten

Soft On Sin

From time to time I have a conversation with someone who thinks that the Episcopal Church is too soft on sin. The general spirit of these conversations is that we talk too much about love and forgiveness. The suggestion is that we need to come down harder on sin. All of the scandals in the Church today are often attributed to the clergy not being tough enough on sin. The feeling is that if people have truly committed their lives to Christ, then they can't be tempted. Those who yield to temptation have not had enough faith and are negligent in their spiritual duties.

One man suggested that the Church should be more like the school he attended. There was an honor code in that school and anyone who couldn't cut it was thrown out of the school. He suggested that any bishop, priest, or lay person who couldn't "cut it" as a Christian should be thrown out of the Church. In his words, "The Church then could be a pure example to the rest of the world. The Church would stand for something. The world will see the Church as a holy place filled with holy people led by bishops and priests beyond reproach. People will be clamoring to get in the doors."

It was Archbishop Temple who first said, "The Church is a hospital for sinners. It is not a showcase for saints." Sadly, there are those who want the Church to be a private club for those who can give the illusion of being the elect. It is difficult for us to reconcile being redeemed with acts of sin. I think all of us would like to believe that once one is baptized, confirmed, saved, committed to Christ, filled with the Holy Spirit, and particularly if they have been ordained, they will be inoculated against sin. It is precisely this attitude that makes it difficult to accept the fact that "All sin. All come short of the Glory of God." (*Romans 3:23*) Even the people we have set apart for holy purposes — popes, bishops, priests, deacons, wardens, vestry — all of us yield to temptation, and like St. Paul writes, "We do those things we do not want to do, and we leave undone those things we would do." (*Romans 7:15*)

The Baptismal Service holds up the ideals of what it is to be a Christian. One of the most critical vows in the Baptismal Service is "When you fall into sin, will you repent and return to the Lord?" (*BCP 304*) Notice it does not say "if you sin." It says "when you sin." From the moment we make our first commitment to Christ, we both hold up the Christian ideal and make provision for repentance when we fail to live up to that ideal.

I have looked into the tear-streaked faces of people kneeling before the Bishop for Confirmation. I have known their resolve to begin again, to live the Christian ideal. I have heard the sobs of some of those same people when they failed to do so. Brides and grooms have pledged their fidelity with all the determination they can muster. I have ministered to their failure. I have heard priests and bishops in solemn ceremonies commit to "pattern their own lives and that of their families,"(*BCP 532*) and I have shared in their common failure.

The Christian ideal is not weakened by acknowledging our common failure to live up to those ideals. We strive for perfection while living daily with our failure to achieve it. The prescription for failure is not to give up, nor is the prescription to pretend that there are any of us who have mastered the Christian ideal. By far, such pretense is the greater mockery! The prescription for failure is repentance, not denial. There is healing in repentance. Through repentance we are given the opportunity to begin again and again. God does not give up on us, and we must not give up on each other. If we can be that type of Church, the type of Church that welcomes sinners and makes the forgiveness of God real to all, be they bishop or lay person, then I do believe people will be clamoring to get into our doors.

Chapter Eleven

No Human Is Worthy

When did all of this begin? Maybe it started with the televangelist scandals. The names and circumstances are all so familiar. Now the scandal mongers appear to be having a field day. Supreme Court nominees' private lives and characters are laid open to national curiosity. The secret sins of presidential candidates become front page news. Cabinet appointees are given microscopic examinations until finally an act of sin is discovered.

The Church of Jesus Christ is no less guilty of this tabloid journalism. Constant are the scandalous news stories of the sins of Bishops, candidates for Bishops and priests, and the candidates for other positions in the Church.

A teacher in a church school is told she can no longer teach because it has been discovered she was a "go-go dancer" fifteen years ago. A background check on a candidate for a rector's job reveals that she is a recovering alcoholic. Twenty years of sobriety not being enough, she is removed from the list of candidates.

It is rumored that some bishops in our Church hire private detectives to do complete background checks on candidates for positions in their dioceses. Contrary to the prayer of the Psalmist, we live in a time when the sins of one's youth are not only remembered but may be recanted in detail on the front page of secular and church press.

Please understand, I am not arguing against accountability. We each must be held accountable before God and before one another. The Church must never bless that which Jesus has come to redeem. I also realize fully that actions have consequences. Every one of us lives daily with the consequences of our actions, our good choices and our bad ones, our sins of commission and omission. The consequences are ever present. Even the consequences of the secrets we carry, hoping the truth will never be revealed, weigh upon us. We do not keep secrets; our secrets keep us!

I should like to work for a rediscovery of repentance and forgiveness. We have become a society and a church engaged in a witch hunt. Any person who steps forward for a position of leadership is scrutinized for acts of sin. Then, in utter amazement, we are shocked and disgusted to find that a human being has a past and has committed sins. Our only challenge is to discern which of the sins will suit our purpose and make good tabloid journalism.

The plumb line by which we measure sin is not the standard of God, but the tabloid press. The sins of Hollywood — sex, drugs, money, and booze are unforgivable. The sins of the polite neighborhood that are every bit as destructive of people's lives are ignored. Is the workaholic spouse who ignores wife and children in pursuit of achievement a better candidate for high office than the person with twenty years of sobriety? Is the manipulative person who controls his spouse and children with anger, guilt, money, and other control tactics any more qualified for high office than the adulterer who has repented of his ways and been faithful to his marriage since doing so? Is the competitive person who destroys the lives of others with gossip, slander, and innuendo any more virtuous than the thief who has repented and sinned that sin no more?

The writer of *First John* makes it clear that all wrongdoing is sin. He also makes it clear that all of us have sinned. Any person who says he has not sinned is a liar.

Martin Luther stated, "The true sign of a sinner is his inability to see his own sin." Since we all are sinners, then we all desperately need a Church that will make forgiveness real and repentance a true act of reconciliation. We need a Church where the sins of the past are put away and remembered no more.

In no way should we advocate a cheap grace. As a nation we have not been able to forgive Richard Nixon, Jim Bakker, or Jimmy Swaggart simply because we do not believe their repentance is real. I believe, however, when repentance is real, so must be our forgiveness.

Who is worthy? The answer — none is worthy; no, not one of us. Moses, David, Solomon, Mary Magdalene, Simon Peter, Augustine — none were worthy; not a single person in high office in church or State today is worthy.

At ordinations when the congregation is asked, "Is he/she worthy?" I am tempted to shout, "No, but are they repentant?" Because none is worthy; no, not one, the need for the Church to offer genuine forgiveness and model authentic repentance is all the more critical — even urgent!

The tabloid justice we presently dispense can only lead us further from the ministry Jesus entrusted to us. If we can't learn from Jesus, maybe the words of *Othello*, Act III, Scene III, might help us —

> Good name in man or woman, dear my Lord, is the immediate jewel of their souls: Who steals my purse steals trash; tis something, nothing; twas mine, tis his, and has been slave to thousands; but he who filches from me my good name robs me of that which not enriches him, and makes me poor indeed.

Chapter Twelve

Slander Is So Easy

The Nightly News reported that a physician has now developed a security camera for marketing. This camera will be placed in all examining rooms, classrooms, offices of attorneys, counselors, dentists, and priests. Any person who comes into contact with people in an atmosphere of confidentiality can purchase these cameras. The camera will take still pictures at periodic intervals. It can be opened only by a bonded security company. Its purpose is to protect the professional from accusations of wrong doing. The photos would dispute any allegations.

Don't you find it interesting that a video camera brought the Rodney King case to light? Now, police officers across the country have video cameras mounted on their dash boards to protect them from false allegations. A popular Roman Catholic Cardinal is accused of molesting an Altar Boy. In the news, the Cardinal is tried, found guilty, and convicted. Then the man withdraws his accusations. The damage to the good Cardinal is done. What is his recourse? Can he ever completely get his good name back?

Now caring professionals are beginning to fight back. In Waco, Texas, a Board of Deacons wanted to get rid of their preacher. They accused him of having an extramarital affair with one of the members. They fired him. He fought back by suing the Board of Deacons individually and corporately for slander. They settled with him out of court.

Perhaps a whole new field of litigation has now been opened up. Gossip, slander, and character assassination in the past were thought of as the hobbies of the idle. Today, they have devastating consequences. Each time these accusations are given front page in the news of church or State, I believe that both our nation and our church are injured.

Is it coincidental that whatever President is in office, their lives are subjected to microscopic examination, including the sins of their youth? This public airing of accusations and innuendoes harms the people being attacked, the work they have been chosen to perform, and ultimately all of us.

Character assassination has become the primary weapon in the arsenal of whoever the opposition happens to be. Now everyone who has a public life has to seek out "Spin Doctors" and "Damage Control Experts" to protect his or her character and the welfare of their families.

Our hearts and our ministries must continually be open to those who are the real victims of people who abuse their power. At the same time, re-reading of the story of Joseph and the wife of his Egyptian master (*Genesis 39*) might refresh our memories on other possibilities for accusations.

Perhaps some attention needs to be given to the motives of those who make the accusations. I have grown weary of hearing each political party hold up the other's "dirty laundry" in an effort to discredit the entire party. And what of those who have suddenly discovered that pain they suffered decades ago could be softened by several million dollars? The motives of the accusers need to be considered to give balance. Is the problem the real problem or is it a symbol of something else?

The sad truth is that it is all too easy. Any one of us can start a rumor about any person we choose this very day.

We need only to get two or three people to begin repeating it. If we can make the accusation take place ten, twenty, or thirty years ago it becomes all the more difficult to dispute.

Gossip and accusations are not new. The fifth chapter of *I Timothy* speaks plainly to those who have too much time on their hands and are given more to idle gossip than to good work. The writer also lays down the rule in the nineteenth verse, "Never accept any accusation against an elder except on the evidence of two or three witnesses." A witness is someone who saw it or heard it for themselves. A witness is not a person who had it repeated to them, imagined it, concluded it, or invented it.

It appears that the scriptural instruction is to give one another the benefit of the doubt. Unless we are an eye witness ourselves, or personally know two or three eye witnesses, then conjecture probably needs to be dismissed for exactly that.

The motives of the tabloids are obvious. There is fame and fortune in the public display of garbage! The motives of those who want to pass on harmful information about our brothers and sisters in Christ need equal examination. Giving folks the benefit of the doubt may seem like a naive way to live for some. Personally, I prefer to do so. It seems much closer to the Spirit of Christ than does the mindless chatter of the idle.

I love this country and my Church too much to give it over to the destructive work of the tabloids — professional and amateur. That there are legitimate cases of abuse of power on the part of helping professionals is a sad commentary on those individuals. That every helping professional in the country is now having to operate out of a defensive posture is a sad commentary on all of us.

Chapter 13

Please Don't Make A Liar Out Of Me!

I have been hearing private confessions almost from the day I was ordained to the priesthood. I made my first private confession in seminary. Each time I have granted absolution, I have concluded with these words from the prayer book, "The Lord has put away all your sins." (*BCP 448*)

I have taught that when a priest pronounces absolution, the penitent is being restored to the full fellowship of the community. I have taught that when the priest says, "God forgives you," he is also saying —

> I forgive you, the Altar Guild forgives you, the choir forgives you, the men's group forgives you, the acolytes forgive you, the Women of the Church forgive you, the diocese forgives you, the National Church forgives you, the entire Anglican Communion forgives you, and the Church Catholic on earth and in heaven forgives you. Now go, sin no more. You are fully restored to the body. You are completely reconciled to God and to His Church.

I have taught further that we in the Church should treat one another as though we had just stepped out of the confessional. Who knows? We might have just done that very thing. Clearly, Jesus has given to His Church the power to forgive sins. (*John 20:22*ff) This power does not, however, manifest itself only in the reciting of the words of absolution. Forgiveness has to be manifested in people's lives. Only the Church can make the forgiveness of God real. If you and I don't treat one another in a forgiving manner, then forgiveness remains only an ideology.

Now granted, we are becoming a church driven by fear and suspicion. What must be recognized is that in the process, we are making a mockery out of the very Gospel we profess.

Consider what the background checks would reveal about some well known Biblical leaders. These would not prove to be good insurance risks for positions of leadership in the Church. Noah was a drunk; Moses a murderer, David an adulterer, Solomon a materialist, Mary Magdalene a prostitute, Paul a murderer, and Augustine was eaten up by his own lusts.

Today there are Christians with power-filled ministries who don't quite qualify under the insurance regulations. The prison ministry of Charles Colson and the ministry of our own Archbishop need to be called into question. Both were burglars — Charles Colson for Watergate, George Carey for breaking into a box car and stealing a Bible. I have known the power-filled ministries of lay people, priests, and Bishops who have come to terms with their own devils and are allowing God to use their weakness for His strength.

I find it interesting that as we study the lives of those whom we would call saints, we realize that they did not grow in a sense of their own goodness but with even more penitence. Those whom we would call holy accused themselves all the more of their sinfulness. St. Peter asked to be crucified upside down because he did not feel worthy to die in the same way as his Lord. St. Francis of Assisi asked to be removed from his wooded cot to die on the floor because he did not feel worthy to meet his Lord in the comfort of a bed.

I have been holding up the Church as a community of reconciliation and forgiveness for well over two decades. I have taught that it is a place where one's sins are forgiven and put away never to be remembered again. **I have stated emphatically that the Episcopal Church is the Church for those people who do not feel they are good enough to belong to any other church.** I have taught that God can take our mistakes and sins of the past and use them as building blocks for the future. I have prayed with folks and asked God to take garbage and turn it into gold.

I fear that the current atmosphere in the Church is to give the Seal of Confession over to background checks, private detectives and vindictive slander. The Church of Jesus Christ, which offered the only hope in this world for repentant men and women, is becoming the exclusive property of those who can successfully pretend to have no sins worthy of note. I am going to continue to hear private confessions, and I am going to continue to tell folks that God forgives them and that He will remember their sins no more. My appeal must go out to other repentant sinners who believe in the grace of God. Please don't make a liar out of me or any priest who still believes in the Seal of Confession and the Sacrament of Penance.

Chapter Fourteen

Jesus Is A Pain Doctor

I spend almost every day listening to people in pain. I have been doing this for twenty-four years of ministry. Often the pain is self-inflicted. There is the wife caught in adultery and rocked with pain. I have been to prison to visit a man convicted of causing injury to another. I have known the suffering of the businessman who has been accused of improper conduct. I have walked my fellow clergy through failed marriages and the humiliation of divorce. I have watched the tears of the young professional who realized only too late that he had sacrificed marriage and family for career. I have heard the sobs of the most arrogant and self-sufficient among us as their sins brought them to their knees.

Sometimes the pain is not self-inflicted. There are the victims of incest and rape. There are the children trying to come to terms with the pain that their mother and father will never again live together. I have listened to the painful confusion of those trying to make sense out of another's act of suicide or homicide. I have watched the torment of young men and women confused by their sexual identities. And yes, since the two sadly seem to go together in our minds, I have seen the terror on the faces of those diagnosed with a death sentence.

Whether the pain has been actively self-inflicted, the result of one's passivity, or because one is in every sense of the word a victim, the pain is real! Day in and day out for twenty-four years I have listened to the pain of others. I have witnessed their suffering. I have known their hurt.

It is inconceivable that anyone would go into a hospital ward and lecture a person dying of lung cancer on the evils of smoking. Or who would say to the person with a destroyed liver, you are getting what you deserve for all those years of drinking. Would we lecture anyone in physical distress on the cause of their suffering? Can you imagine saying to any of them, "Suffer! You are getting what you deserve. You did it to yourself!"

If the gospels make anything clear, it is that Jesus is a pain doctor. Think on His words to the woman caught in adultery. The self-righteous would have stoned her to death. Read again the account of the woman at the well. Feel His compassion for the loneliness and isolation of Zacheus. Hear His words of forgiveness to the thief on the cross. Jesus is a pain doctor.

For twenty-four years I have been telling people confronted with the consequences of their own sins and the sins of others that God forgives them. I have been pointing them toward Jesus. I have held up the cross as the ultimate outpouring of God's love and forgiveness on our every sin. To those whose suffering is self-inflicted, I have said, "God forgives you; God can put this behind you; now you must forgive yourself." And to those suffering at the sins of others I have urged, "For your soul's sake, you must forgive them as God forgives. You have to put this behind you. Learn from this. Jesus is a pain doctor. He is right in the middle of your pain."

The task of all Christians is to point to Jesus. Those who are suffering even from self-inflicted wounds need to be pointed to Jesus. It is imperative, however, that those of us who point others to Jesus must do so with the same love, compassion, and forgiveness that **is** Jesus! Those in pain need this. We must settle for nothing less. Jesus is a pain doctor. Whenever we come to terms with the consequences of our own sins and the pain we cause others, there is no other we can rely on. He is the only physician who can help us. There is only one pain doctor!

Chapter Fifteen

Tough Love

I confess that some of the most stress-filled days of my life have been those days I had to exercise tough love. Tough love calls us to confront an unacceptable behavior in another person. In extreme cases, tough love requires us to use the tools of discipline and end the relationship.

The scriptures make it clear that the purpose of Christian discipline is always to bring the unrepentant to repentance. Christian discipline is not to be used for the purpose of punishment, revenge, or public humiliation. The mission of the Church and all Christians is reconciliation. Christian love, which on occasion must take on the qualities of tough love, always seeks to reconcile the unrepentant to God and to the Christian family.

Every parent can identify with those occasions when they have had to use the tools of discipline to confront an unacceptable behavior in a child or teen. Only an abusive person would use these tools to punish or injure the child's self-image or self-confidence. Discipline serves to confront unacceptable behavior and lead the person to correct their course of action. This is the essence of Christian repentance. The goal of repentance is to turn around and begin to go in the opposite direction. Only the dark side of our personalities takes delight in another person's downfall. It takes a very mean-spirited person to take delight in calling attention to another person's sinful behavior. Yet if we really love one another, we are called to intervene in destructive life patterns.

The Christian will always do so for the purpose of bringing another to repentance. Never will we consciously do so to embarrass them or punish them. Such occasions have always come at great pain to me, after sleepless nights, and with much prayer. Some of my happiest acts have been to pronounce absolution over those who have so corrected their behavior and to celebrate their new ministries with them.

The exercise of tough love for the purposes of bringing another to repentance cannot be learned in a book. It has to be modeled for us. I have been fortunate enough to sit at the feet of my fellow clergy and bishops who have, with great care and pain, exercised this discipline over others. By the same token, I have watched other clergy, bishops, and lay people use their authority not for the purpose of bringing another to repentance, but to injure, hurt, get revenge, destroy, or publicly humiliate the offender.

To this day I treasure those moments in my life and my ministry when wise people — clergy, bishops, and lay people have loved me enough to confront destructive behavior they saw in me. Intuitively, I have always known when they were on target and that they really loved me. Moreover, I have always known when there were those who did not have my best interest at heart, but only wanted to control, manipulate, embarrass or otherwise injure me.

Bringing another to repentance is a two-fold process. Intervening in the behavior to bring one to repentance is the first step. Being there to celebrate their repentance with them is the second part of the process. This second step is the most telling step of all. Those whose motives are pure and directed to reconciliation will be there to celebrate our new resolve with us. They will rejoice in our repentance and bless our new life. They will continue to be a vital and supportive part of our new commitments.

Christians are to be known by their love. Christian love always seeks what is best for one another and that which is best for the Church. So called "love" which seeks only to punish, injure, humiliate, or gain revenge against another may disguise itself as love, but it is not. It may be some form of love, but it is not Christian love.

Chapter 16

God's Message Is Never Anonymous!

Have you ever been asked to be another person's messenger? There is usually a bit of unpleasant news that someone wants to have delivered to another person. They don't want to deliver it themselves so they ask you to do it for them.

Through the years I have learned that this is a foolish thing to do. I have yet to be able to do it successfully. Often, I have felt it was my responsibility as the Rector or a person's priest or friend to deliver the message. Often the message was for the recipient's own good and one they needed to hear. Sometimes it was to let them know that there was a rumor or accusation about their behavior and they needed to know what people were saying about them. Sometimes the messages were so mundane as to be ridiculous. There have been other times that the messages came in the form of something close to slander and would have best been deposited in the circular file.

It is absolutely amazing how folks aren't just delighted to hear what someone else has told us to tell them. It's surprising that we can't open ourselves to hearing what some people are saying about us or to the latest derogatory rumor about us on the gossip circuit. How shocking it is to learn that people respond defensively to an attack on their character, behavior, or moral values. I think the frustration and anger becomes even more intense when it is cloaked in a cloud of anonymity and being conveyed through a messenger.

The United States Constitution (*Amendment 6*) guarantees the accused the right to face their accuser. It is a right that is based upon some solid Biblical teachings about how we are to relate to one another. The Bible says nothing about us being the messengers of innuendo, rumor, accusations or slander. The Scripture directs rather that when we are an eye witness to a brother or sister committing acts of sin we go directly to that person and confront them with their behavior. There are no instructions about sending another in our place.

I asked a Bishop friend of mine what he does with the anonymous letters he gets accusing his clergy of misbehavior. He said that he puts them in an envelope and sends them directly to the clergy being accused. They are of no value to the Bishop and if they aren't true then they are of no value to the priest either.

Another person told me that they never give written letters of recommendation. They felt they were more free then to be honest. I responded that they were also more free to be slanderous. I should think that we Christians would insist on written recommendations and that nothing be written on the recommendation that we do not know to be true and that we would unashamedly place our signature on. I think the whole business of needing to protect our sources and insure anonymity for those who would do another person harm flies right in the face of the Biblical principles guiding our relationships with one another. Such is obviously contrary to the rights guaranteed each one of us under the *Constitution of the United States*.

We really are called to be messengers for only One. As messengers for God, we will carry the Good News. When we have delivered our message, it will be received with gratitude. The gospel gives Life. The gospel brings forgiveness. The gospel is healing and reconciling. The gospel washes away our sins and shortcomings and gives us a promise for a new tomorrow. The gospel builds people up, it does not tear them down. Such a gospel does not put us on the defensive. No, both the message and the messenger will always be received with gratitude. We need only decide whose messenger we will be and whether or not the message is the one He would have us deliver.

Chapter Seventeen

Forgive and Forget

Mrs. Cunningham lived next door to us when I was a child. Every spring the yard around her house was filled with tulips. They were absolutely beautiful. One afternoon, my neighborhood friends and I decided we would go into Mrs. Cunningham's yard and pick some big beautiful bouquets for our mothers. You can imagine our confusion when we discovered that these bouquets did not bring our mothers joy, but distress. It was not until I was forced to confront Mrs. Cunningham, confess what I had done, and see the tears streaming down her cheeks that I came to terms with the pain my actions had caused another human being.

This was also my first lesson in the irreversible nature of sin. The act had been done and there was nothing I could do to put it back the way it was before. The flower was off the stem and no amount of wishing otherwise could put it back. Words once spoken or written cannot be retrieved. Missed opportunities seldom present themselves a second time. We can't erase, we can't undo, we can't go back, it will never again be the same.

Often, in trying to reconcile couples after a break in the relationship one will say, "I will never be able to love them in the same way again." My response is, "Good. You need to learn to love in a new way. You need to incorporate this pain into a different kind of relationship so that this cannot happen again."

What is the good news in the face of the irreversible damage done by our acts of sin? The Bible assures us that if we will confess our sins, God is faithful and just to forgive them. The Bible also assures us that God develops amnesia. He forgets them. God remembers our sins no more! (*Isaiah 43:25*)

We humans are not so wired. By the grace of God we can forgive. We do not forget. So what does it mean to forgive and forget? We must learn how to do both.

Recently, I was listening to a man tell me how another person had hurt him. His pain was real, his hurt justified in my mind. And then I learned the incident that he was describing took place thirty years ago! Thirty years ago, yet he was describing it with such force one would have thought it had just happened. Can you imagine the toll all these years of bitterness have taken on this man's health? I began to study his face and could see how the resentment he had nurtured all these years had even taken a toll on his demeanor. And what of his soul, can you imagine how calloused it has become?

One of my favorite stories is about the farmer who had a cat that he loved dearly. One day the cat died and the farmer took it into his backyard to bury it. Lovingly he buried the cat in a shallow grave. To help mark the spot where his cat lay, he left the tail sticking out of the ground.

A few weeks went by, and the farmer went out to the grave to see how his cat was doing. He reached down and pulled the cat up by its tail. The cat didn't look so good! The cat didn't smell so good either! The farmer put the cat back in the grave again leaving the tail out.

As the weeks turned into months, the farmer would periodically go out and pull the cat up by its tail. Each time he did so, the cat looked worse and smelled worse than it did the time before.

To forgive and forget means that we leave the past in the past. As bad as it was at the time, each time we bring it into the present it will look worse and smell worse than it was.

Forget — we are not wired to do so. By the grace of God we can forgive and we can leave the past in the past and not keep bringing it into the present. When we have truly forgiven another person, the past remains the past and the future an opportunity to begin again. God buries our sins, tail and all. We must learn how to do the same.

A few weeks after I had picked Mrs. Cunningham's flowers, I knew she had forgiven me. She asked me to water her flowers while she was on vacation. I had been forgiven. She had decided to forget. I was now in charge of her flowers. I had been restored. We both were healed.

Chapter Eighteen

A New Model For The Divorced Family

Recently, while preaching in another city, a neighboring priest asked me to do a favor for him. "I want you to meet with my ex-wife, my daughter, and me." He continued, "Our daughter is getting married this summer, and we want to do all we can to help her get her marriage started on the right foot."

It was a fascinating ninety minutes. There was little for me to say or do, but I got to witness the love of Jesus in action. In an atmosphere of healing and warmth, these two people tried to help their daughter understand what their marriage failure had taught them. Not one time was there even a hint of blaming, embarrassing, or humiliating the other. Each accepted responsibility for the breakdown in the relationship. Each praised the other for their efforts to salvage it.

The marriage itself had been a textbook case in "Marriage and Family 101." They were married far too young. They had known each other only a few months. They had known almost immediately that they had made a mistake. Both had wanted to cancel or at least postpone the wedding, but the excitement of the wedding itself drove their decision. They were such opposites I wondered how they had ever gotten together to begin with. He took a mistress — the Church, and lost himself in ministry. She took a lover as well — her career. The end was ever so predictable.

I could not help but contrast these two people's efforts to assist their daughter in coming to terms with their divorce with what far too often is the usual behavior for divorced parents. The children more often than I like to admit become the prize in the couple's tug of war. Serious damage is inflicted on the innocent children by one or both parents blaming, criticizing, and attacking the other. Far too often, one or both will try to present themselves to the children as the ideal spouse who was victimized by the other's sins. In their efforts to justify and purify themselves in the eyes of the children, they will lead unrelenting attacks on the character, morals, and sanity of their ex-spouse. No one is injured in this type of tirade but the children!

I don't know if Jesus had divorce in mind when he said, "Love your enemies and pray for those that persecute you." (*Matthew 5:44*)

I have certainly known cases of divorce where those instructions apply. Healing begins when we accept our responsibility for things done and left undone that led to the dissolution of any relationship. Healing begins when we stop blaming and attacking the other in order to justify ourselves. Healing begins when we forgive ourselves and forgive the other.

Divorced parents who really love their children have everything to gain by focusing on each other's good qualities. Divorced parents who really love their children will each wish the other the best and want every good thing for the person with whom they shared the miracle of childbirth. Divorced parents who really love their children will realize that nursing their anger and hurt destroys the very people they profess to love. Divorced parents who try to justify themselves by destroying the other in the children's eyes end up damaging these little ones and their possibilities for a successful relationship and marriage.

Divorced parents with children will be brought together throughout their lives for many occasions. Divorced Christians are given the opportunity to model the love of Jesus for their children and all those around them. This is a unique ministry that few would choose, but one to which half the adult population must respond. It is a real opportunity for us to "manifest in our lives that which we profess with our lips."

It is a Christian ministry. It is a ministry that will bring healing to everyone who has been touched by divorce. Failure to accept this ministry means only that both parents lose, but the children pay the greatest price of all.

Chapter Nineteen

Cheap Grace

When I was teenager I had a "friend" who was very competitive. He was constantly setting me up for his manipulated victories. Often, in order to win or get one up on me, he would sneak up on my blind side and do something to embarrass me. After he had his laugh and scored his point, he would say, "I'm sorry." After a while, I began to realize that he was not sorry. He only wanted to get back into my good graces so that he could keep the contest going.

Genuine repentance is the prerequisite for forgiveness. Simply saying "I'm sorry" so that we can cover all our bases and keep the contest going is not genuine repentance. The Spiritual Directors remind us that repentance is a four step process.

Step One - Responsibility

By periodically doing a thorough examination of conscience, we become aware of our sins of thought, word, deed, and omission. The critical moment in this step is when we can accept responsibility for our **own** behavior. What we have done and left undone were our decisions, our choices, no one else's fault. In the words of the old Mass, "Through my own fault, my own fault, my **own** most grievous fault."

Step Two - Contrition

Contrition is genuine grief over our sins. We regret the pain they have brought ourselves and others. We genuinely wish that it had been otherwise. We recall the pain, and the pain strengthens our resolve not to repeat the sin again.

Step Three - Confession

When possible we need to go to the person we have injured and ask their forgiveness. If such a confession is going to cause harm to that person or innocent people around that person then such a confession may be ill-advised. It may actually be a self-serving act on our part.

Just as there is cheap grace, there can be a cheap confession. Such a confession leaves another person in agony, but allows us to walk away guilt-free. Such self-serving confessions could be described as a "cheap shot." We need, however, to hear ourselves say that we are sorry. Confessing our sins to another and hearing ourselves recite our acts of sin is a part of the healing of repentance. It is not required for God's forgiveness, but the therapeutic value for ourselves cannot be underestimated. A Spiritual Director can give us words of wisdom, counsel, and comfort that can help us with our resolve.

Step Four - Amendment

Again, if it is possible to make restitution to the person injured without causing harm to that person or innocent people around them, then this needs to be done. Amendment of Life involves a plan of action that will remove us from the temptation, gain treatment, counsel, and support which will assist us in our resolve. This fourth step of repentance is the acid test of its validity.

Dietrich Bonhoeffer coined the phrase "cheap grace" to describe those who sought forgiveness without repentance. He described it as a grace we pour on ourselves. To preach forgiveness without requiring repentance would be a form of cheap grace. To baptize without requiring the candidates to make a commitment to the disciplines of the Church is cheap grace. To receive communion without first making our confession is cheap grace. To seek the grace of God without paying the cost of being a disciple is cheap grace. To try to live the life of a Christian without being willing to submit to the Lordship of Christ is cheap grace.

The grace of God is amazing. It is most amazing to those who have come to terms with their own sins, gone through the process of repentance, and experienced forgiveness. Forgiveness without repentance is a grace that we pour on ourselves. It is no more satisfying than the halfhearted apology of my childhood friend, “I’m sorry.” The grace that God wants to pour upon us came at a great price. Such a grace is anything but cheap.

Chapter Twenty

Forgiveness Without Restoration Is Empty

The Parable of the Prodigal Son is often presented as a lesson in forgiveness. It is not. It is a story about restoration. The elder brother who kept all the ordinances and had done as his father wanted him to do would not have objected nearly as much if the issue were simply one of forgiveness. Oh yes, we can certainly understand the importance of forgiving an offender. We need to do that as much for ourselves as for them. What set the eldest son off was not the fact that his father could forgive the sins of his brother. What set him off was the fact that the father restored the son to his rightful place in the family. Not only was he restored to his position with all of the rights and privileges he had abused, but the father gave him a party and poured additional honor upon him.

I should like to contend that it is not forgiveness that causes us to break with teachings of Jesus on reconciliation, it is restoration. Forgiving and forgetting can be very difficult for us, but by God's grace we can exercise them. It is very difficult to take exception with restoring a person spiritually. To restore folks physically to their former rights and privileges takes an extra measure of grace on our part. To not only restore a penitent, but to pour additional honors on them feels like adding insult to injury.

The Church may not be doing any better job with restoration than the world. Gone are the days that we brand a person with a scarlet letter or some other mark of degradation, but very much alive is our want to forever categorize people according to their past sins. Those who have broken the laws of the state and have a criminal record know how difficult it is to be restored to society. That record follows them wherever they go. Their debt to society is not paid in full on the day of their release. Most will pay the rest of their lives. There will be no ring, no robe, no fatted calf for them.

In the Church I have often had to come to the defense of those who have objected to persons serving on the vestry, being a lay reader, serving the chalice, being recommended for ordination, or some other leadership ministry in the Church because of a past sin. The argument is that they are not worthy. They are not good enough. They should not be allowed to have that honor or privilege.

Forgiveness without restoration is just as incomplete as is forgiveness without true repentance. If a person has truly repented of their sin and amended their life to follow again the commandments of God, then the words of absolution will be as a noisy gong or clanging cymbal if they are not followed with restoration. The intent of the Christian sacrament of Reconciliation has always been full restoration. "Those who, because of notorious sins, had been separated from the body of the faithful were reconciled by penitence and forgiveness, and **restored** to the fellowship of the Church." (*BCP 265*)

What kind of ending would it have been if the Father had only forgiven the prodigal son? "Yes, I can see that your repentance is real so I forgive you, but you are going to have to sleep in the servant's quarters. You have already blown your inheritance so don't expect to receive anything else from me. You are forgiven, but I will never let you forget what you have done. You are forgiven, but you have forfeited all your rights and privileges as a member of this family."

Thank God that is not the way Jesus ended this parable. "Bring out a robe — the best one — and put it on him; put a ring on his finger and sandals on his feet. And get the fatted calf and kill it, and let us eat and celebrate, for this son of mine was dead and is alive again; he was lost and is found. And they began to celebrate." (*Luke 15:23*)

The eldest son would have held his righteous superiority over the prodigal. Jesus did not allow that to happen in the parable. You and I must not allow that to happen in the Church. Forgiveness without restoration is an empty forgiveness. It is not the forgiveness of God, and it must never be the forgiveness modeled by Christian people in His Church.

Chapter Twenty-One

The Forgiveness Business

Recently two convicted murderers have been put to death in our nation. Both had confessed to their crimes. They had committed terrible atrocities on their victims. Those they murdered had suffered agonizing deaths. These two also died terrible deaths. One was executed in the gas chamber and the other by hanging. Both suffered several moments before they died.

Now I have a confession. In light of what they did to their victims, there was a part of me that was delighted to know that they also had painful deaths. Albeit, it may be a dark part of me, but the thought at least crossed my mind — "they got what they deserved!" Justice had been served.

There is a part of me that still thinks that justice has something to do with fairness. An eye for an eye and a tooth for a tooth; now that would be fair. Yet every day my concept of fairness is challenged. Some folks I know have been visited with suffering, but they are good people. They don't deserve to suffer. It is not fair.

On the other hand, there are those who have been given wealth, power, and privilege who I think don't deserve that either. By my standards, they are selfish people. It is not fair.

Even in the Church, we sometimes think that ministry, honor, and privilege have something to do with justice. "Why are you letting him/her read the scriptures, serve the chalice, be a member of the vestry, or apply for Holy Orders? Don't you know about their past sins? They are reprobates. They don't deserve that honor or privilege."

I worked for a bishop for several years who used to leave me with this parting blessing, "I hope you get every thing that you have coming to you."

I want to make a distinction and then I want to offer a definition. First, the distinction. The Criminal Justice System is not in the forgiveness business. Actions have consequences. The civil and criminal laws of the land are clear. If we violate those laws then there will be repercussions; there will be punishment.

The Criminal Justice System is not in the forgiveness business, but the Church of Jesus Christ is! When we compare ourselves against God's standard then clearly we all have sinned, we all are violators, we all have fallen short.

That brings us to the definition. Let me offer a theological definition of justice. Justice means that the consequences of every evil thought I have ever had, every malicious word I have uttered, every hurtful deed I have committed, and all the good that I could have done but failed to do will fall upon no one but me. Now that is justice.

In light of that definition of justice, none of us wants justice. None of us wants exactly what we deserve.

In the penitential services in our prayer book, we do not pray for justice. We pray for mercy. We pray for forgiveness. And, we pray that we might be restored.

The good news is that when a penitent truly repents, when a person is genuinely grieved over their sins, when a person confesses his or her sins, when a person amends his or her life in such a way that they will not fall victim to that sin again, God forgives us. Not only does He forgive us, but He restores us to our former place in the family. We are His sons and daughters. Our inheritance is restored.

The Criminal Justice System is not in the forgiveness business. That is the business of the Church of Jesus Christ. There are some who have forgotten this distinction. There are some who would have us punish the sinners and in their vindictiveness never let them forget their sins. Such is not the message of Jesus.

God does not give us justice. God does not give us exactly what we deserve. God forgives the penitent and restores them to their rightful place in the family.

My brothers and sisters in Christ Jesus, if that is what God does for us, can we afford to do less for one another? The Church is the only community in the world today that offers this kind of hope to the penitent. Here, you can begin again. Here, your sins will be remembered no more. For those who are truly repentant, this is the community of reconciliation. In this household, all penitents are fully restored!